YOU CHOOSE BOOKS™

THE BATTLE OF BULL RUN

An Interactive History Adventure

by Allison Lassieur

Consultant:

Mark Snell, PhD
Associate Professor of History/Director
George Tyler Moore Center for the Study of the Civil War
Shepherd University
Shepherdstown, West Virginia

You Choose Books are published by Capstone Press,
151 Good Counsel Drive, P.O. Box 669, Mankato, Minnesota 56002.
www.capstonepub.com

Books published by Capstone Press are manufactured with paper
containing at least 10 percent post-consumer waste.

Library of Congress Cataloging-in-Publication Data
Lassieur, Allison.
    The Battle of Bull Run: an interactive history adventure / by Allison Lassieur.
    p. cm. — (You choose books)
    Summary: "Describes the events surrounding the Battle of Bull Run during the
Civil War. The reader's choices reveal the historical details from the perspective of a
Union soldier, a Confederate soldier, and a civilian"— Provided by publisher.
    Includes bibliographical references and index.
    ISBN-13: 978-1-4296-2011-6 (hardcover)
    ISBN-10: 1-4296-2011-0 (hardcover)
    ISBN-13: 978-1-4296-3458-8 (paperback)
    ISBN-10: 1-4296-3458-8 (paperback)
    1. Bull Run, 1st Battle of, Va., 1861 — Juvenile literature. I. Title. II. Series.
E472.18.L38 2009
973.7'31 — dc22   2008007555

Editorial Credits
Angie Kaelberer, editor; Juliette Peters, set designer; Patrick D. Dentinger, book designer;
    Danielle Ceminsky, illustrator; Wanda Winch, photo researcher

Photo Credits
Getty Images Inc./Stock Montage, 65; Library of Congress, cover, 11, 12, 14, 23, 31, 44, 46, 51,
56, 58, 61, 67, 70, 77, 79, 98, 105; Mary Evans Picture Library, 41, 100; National Archives and
Records Administration (NARA), 20, 89, 90; North Wind Picture Archives, 6, 93; Painting by
Don Troiani (c)2008/www.historicalimagebank.com, 38, 52, 85; SuperStock Inc./SuperStock,
103

Printed in the United States of America in Stevens Point, Wisconsin.
042013
007301R

TABLE OF CONTENTS

About Your Adventure

YOU are living in the United States in 1861. The country is fighting a civil war. Which side should you support? What will happen to you?

In this book, you'll explore how the choices people made meant the difference between life and death. The events you'll experience happened to real people.

Chapter One sets the scene. Then you choose which path to read. Follow the directions at the bottom of each page. The choices you make will change your outcome. After you finish one path, go back and read the others for new perspectives and more adventures.

*YOU CHOOSE the path
you take through history.*

Slaves provided the huge amount of labor needed to grow and harvest sugarcane and other crops in the South.

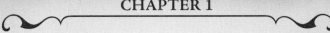

A Torn Country

It's summer 1861. All over the United States, cities and towns are unusually quiet. You know it's not because of the hot weather. A few weeks ago, the Civil War began. No one is really sure what will happen next.

You're not sure why the war started, but you know it has something to do with slavery. For many years, white people in Southern states have owned black slaves. Slave owners say they need the slaves to work the plantations and farms that grow cotton, tobacco, and sugarcane.

7

Turn the page.

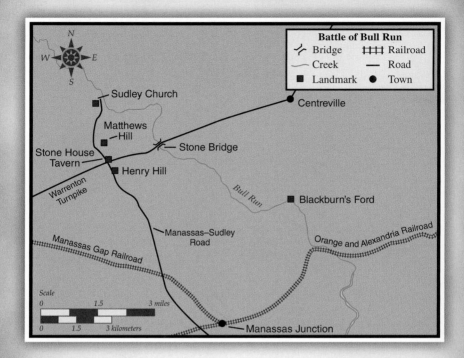

Some people in Northern states think slavery is wrong. But many white Southerners say they have a right to do anything they want, including owning slaves. These Southerners believe the individual states should have the right to make their own laws.

The two sides have argued for years. In late 1860, Northern lawyer Abraham Lincoln was elected president of the United States. Lincoln was against the spread of slavery into the new western territories of the country. His election was the last straw for the Southern states.

One by one, seven states seceded, or withdrew, from the United States. Those states were South Carolina, Mississippi, Florida, Alabama, Georgia, Louisiana, and Texas. These states formed a new country called the Confederate States of America, or the Confederacy.

President Lincoln didn't believe the states had a right to secede. He vowed to make sure the United States stayed together, even if he had to go to war.

Turn the page.

On April 12, 1861, Confederate soldiers fired on Fort Sumter in South Carolina. U.S. soldiers in the fort surrendered the next day.

After the attack on Fort Sumter, Virginia, Arkansas, North Carolina, and Tennessee joined the Confederacy. Soldiers on both the Union and Confederate sides signed up to fight.

The Union Army includes about 35,000 men. The Confederate forces include the Army of the Potomac and the Army of the Shenandoah. Combined, these forces number about 32,000.

For weeks, the Union and Confederate armies have been moving toward Manassas Junction, Virginia. This village is about 30 miles southwest of Washington, D.C. You've never been to Manassas Junction, but you've heard it's an important place.

Early in the morning of April 12, 1861, Confederate cannons fired on Fort Sumter in South Carolina.

Turn the page.

A huge number of weapons were made and stored at the U.S. Armory and Arsenal at Harpers Ferry, Virginia.

Two railroads, the Manassas Gap and the Orange and Alexandria, meet at Manassas Junction. The railroads are a gateway to the Union capitol of Washington, D.C. They also lead to the naval shipyards at Norfolk, Virginia, and the federal arsenal at Harpers Ferry, Virginia.

You know that the army that controls the railroads will have a huge advantage. A battle can't be far behind.

13

➤ *To fight in the Confederate Army, turn to page* **15**.

➤ *To fight in the Union Army, turn to page* **45**.

➤ *To watch the battle as a civilian bystander, turn to page* **71**.

In 1861, Southern men rushed to Richmond, Virginia, to volunteer for the Confederate Army.

CHAPTER 2

FIGHTING FOR THE CONFEDERACY

It's dawn, and you're marching with your regiment. Last night, you boarded a train and left the Confederate capital of Richmond, Virginia. It's hard to believe that just a few weeks ago, you were working beside your father and brothers on your small Virginia farm.

When you heard about the attack on Fort Sumter, you rushed to enlist. Your family doesn't own slaves, but that doesn't matter to you. No Yankee government is going to tell you and other Southerners what to do.

15

Turn the page.

When you arrived at the Richmond capitol building, you were amazed at the crowds. All of the men in the county seemed to be there. Many of the young men in line were your friends.

One of the regiments forming will be part of the Army of the Potomac, commanded by General Pierre Beauregard. The other will be part of the Army of the Shenandoah, led by General Joseph Johnston.

➻*To serve in the Army of the Potomac, go to page **17**.*

➻*To serve in the Army of the Shenandoah, turn to page **28**.*

From Richmond, your regiment took a train to Manassas Junction. Now, you're camped along a nearby creek called Bull Run.

You and your fellow soldiers of the Army of the Potomac don't look much like an army. For one thing, no one has a real uniform. Like you, most men wear a wool jacket, cotton shirt, and wool pants. Your leather boots are nicer than the poor-quality shoes that some of the other soldiers wear. Your extra clothes and blanket are rolled up and tied together at the ends. You carry this blanket roll over your shoulder.

Some soldiers have bags called haversacks filled with food and ammunition. Everyone has a canteen to hold water, plus a rifle or musket and a bayonet.

Turn the page.

A soldier on horseback rides through camp. "General Beauregard is looking for brave men to work as couriers," the rider calls. "Volunteers should go to the general's camp at once."

"What's a courier?" you ask the soldier next to you.

"Couriers deliver messages on horseback during the battle," he replies. "It can be a dangerous job."

➤ *To volunteer to be a courier, go to page 19.*

➤ *To stay with your regiment, turn to page 23.*

You decide to be a courier. You walk to the general's camp on the grounds of a large farm. An aide sees you and motions to follow him.

"Who lives here?" you ask the aide as you reach a tidy farmhouse.

"Wilmer McLean," the aide replies. Inside the farmhouse, General Beauregard and several of his aides look at a map. Beauregard looks up. His dark eyes gleam with intelligence.

"So you want to deliver messages for me, eh?" he asks. You nod, suddenly nervous to be talking to the man who led the attack on Fort Sumter.

You're given a pistol and a fast horse. As you climb into the saddle, you hear the boom of distant cannons. The battle has begun.

Turn the page.

B-1233

General Pierre G. T. Beauregard
was a native of Louisiana and a
Mexican War veteran.

Beauregard rushes from the farmhouse. "Courier," he shouts to you, "come here at once."

Beauregard hands you a piece of paper. "Take this to my commanders on the front lines." You nod, tucking the note into your jacket. Then you and your horse speed toward the cannon fire.

You don't go far before you hear the popping noise of gunfire. Smoke fills the air, making you cough. Bullets whiz past you. You bend low against your horse's neck and urge him forward.

Suddenly several Confederate commanders ride out of the smoke toward you. You pull the note from your pocket and hand it to the nearest one. He reads it quickly, scribbles a reply on the bottom, and hands it back.

Turn the page.

"Take this back to Beauregard at once," he orders. You decide to go back through the woods to avoid the gunfire. Soon you're completely lost. You finally see a clearing in front of you. The farmhouse at last, you think with relief.

You burst from the woods right into a regiment of Union soldiers. They are as startled as you are. You have just one second to make a decision.

→To run away, turn to page **25**.

→To open fire on the soldiers, turn to page **34**.

Blackburn's Ford on Bull Run (shown in 1862) was the setting for a skirmish on July 18, 1861.

You'd rather be an ordinary soldier. Your regiment is positioned on Bull Run creek at an area called Blackburn's Ford. The first thing you notice is a terrible smell.

"What's that?" you ask, holding your nose.

Turn the page.

"A few days ago, there was a skirmish here between the Yankees and some of our soldiers. That smell is the dead bodies," a soldier tells you.

You notice several small mounds covered in mud and swarming with flies. You feel sick. To your shock, the order comes to bury the bodies. No one can stand to get too close. You and the other soldiers do little more than throw a few shovels of dirt on the bodies.

You barely finish when you hear the sound of guns and cannons firing. Your commander orders you to lie down. You don't understand why. The Yankees are coming. Shouldn't you get ready to fight?

➻*To stand up, turn to page 27.*

➻*To follow orders, turn to page 38.*

The Yankees recover from their shock and reach for their weapons. You barely have enough time to dash into the forest. Bullets thump into the trees beside you as you ride for your life. Finally, you make it back to the farmhouse. Right away, Beauregard sends you out with another message.

All afternoon, you dodge bullets and cannon fire as you deliver messages for the general. You and your horse are covered with soot and sweat. You both need water.

You stop at Bull Run. The creek water is brown with mud churned up by thousands of soldiers' boots. You're so thirsty that you don't care. You drop to your stomach and start slurping the water.

Turn the page.

After you drink your fill, you lie there panting. War isn't what you thought it would be. You sit up and look around. No one is here. You could easily slip away and go back to Richmond.

➤*To stay, turn to page 35.*

➤*To desert the army, turn to page 37.*

You enlisted to fight Yankees, not lie on the ground. You stand up, your hand on your rifle. Your commander sees you.

"Get down, soldier!" he yells at you. "Don't you know how to follow orders?"

You can't believe what the officer is telling you to do. What if he tells you not to move when the Yankees do show up to attack? You need to get out of here while you're still alive. Just then, the commander turns his back. Now is your chance.

Turn to page 37.

As you make your way to your regiment, you see General Johnston. You feel confident under his command.

Soon the orders come to march. The march across the rugged country is disorganized. Some units separate from the army and get lost. You wade through creeks up to your hips and trudge over steep hills. You never realized being in the army could be so miserable.

Early on the morning of July 21, your regiment arrives on the battlefield and gets into position. In the distance, you see the Yankees' guns shining in the sunlight. Someone shouts the order to attack, and you rush forward.

You and a few other soldiers drop behind a small mound. You start shooting at every Yankee you see. Soon the air is filled with smoke and the thundering sound of cannons and guns.

You keep loading and shooting. Bullets thump into the ground around you. One of the soldiers beside you slumps down, shot in the chest. You gulp and keep firing.

"Move position!" you hear. Without thinking, you jump up and run. In the confusion, you're separated from your regiment.

The morning turns into afternoon as you shoot, reload, and shoot again. When you run out of bullets, you grab more from the dead bodies scattered around the battlefield. You're thirsty, sweaty, and hungry. Your fingers are swollen and aching from loading and firing your gun again and again.

Turn the page

Ahead, you see a group of Confederate gunners being attacked. You rush to help them. One of the cannoneers appears through the smoke, a look of terror on his face.

"The other cannoneer is dead," he shouts. "I can't fire this alone. I need help." A company of Yankees is rushing toward you.

→ To help the cannoneer, go to page 31.

→ To attack the Yankees, turn to page 43.

Both Confederate and Union soldiers used cannons during the Civil War.

You drop your gun and help. You have no idea what to do, but the cannoneer shouts instructions. You load the cannonball and step back, covering your ears. A huge blast scatters the Yankees.

Turn the page.

As they run off, you look for the cannoneer. He's lying dead on the ground. You try not to think of him as you pick up your gun and rush back into battle. You need to find your regiment.

Soon you spot a few members of your regiment. They're running in the opposite direction from the battle.

"The battle is lost," one man shouts. "We're beat."

"The Yankees have won the day," another says over his shoulder.

Your heart sinks. If the battle is lost, there's no reason to keep fighting. Or is there? You haven't yet heard the order to retreat from a commander.

➻ To run away, go to page 33.

➻ To stay, turn to page 40.

From the looks of things around you, the soldiers are right. Confederate soldiers are streaming away from the battle, running for their lives. One even says that he heard a Yankee commander declare victory. The battle appears to be lost.

You feel discouraged. War isn't what you thought it would be. In the confusion, no one would know if you left the battle and went home.

33

Turn to page 37.

You reach for your pistol and manage to fire one shot. But the Union soldiers are too fast for you, and there are more of them. Before you have a chance to fire again, a bullet rips through your chest. Your last thought is that you did your best to serve the Confederacy.

THE END

To follow another path, turn to page 13.
To read the conclusion, turn to page 101.

You decide to stay and fight. Before you can get up, a shadow passes over you. You're horrified to see that Union soldiers surround you.

The soldiers search you and find the message you are carrying. They also take your weapons, ammunition, and supplies.

"General McDowell will find this information very helpful," one of the Yankees says to you. "And you'll make a fine prisoner of war."

The soldiers push you forward. Soon you arrive at a Union camp. Several other Confederate soldiers are under guard. The Yankees laugh as they add you to the group of prisoners.

Turn the page.

You'll probably be sent to a prisoner of war camp in the North. You don't know what will happen to you, but you know your days as a soldier are over.

THE END

To follow another path, turn to page 13.
To read the conclusion, turn to page 101.

A patch of woods is nearby. You can hide there until you figure out where to go. When you reach the woods, you peek through the trees at the road. You see other soldiers running away. You feel guilty for leaving the army, but at least you're still alive.

As you plod down the road, the sounds of battle grow fainter. Finally, all you can hear is the steps of dozens of other tired, dirty soldiers who have deserted too. You're sick of war. You're going home.

THE END

To follow another path, turn to page 13.
To read the conclusion, turn to page 101.

The 4th Alabama Regiment fought on Henry Hill during the battle.

Dozens of soldiers get up and run, but you follow orders and remain on the ground. You and the rest of the regiment wait. And wait. You stay there all day, while the sounds of the battle come at you from all directions. That afternoon, you're at last given orders to move.

You cross Bull Run and move quickly down the road. Soldiers are shouting, "The Yankees are retreating!"

Great news! At first, you are ordered to prepare to attack the retreating Union forces. You grip your gun, ready to fight. Then the order comes to move back. You can't believe it, but you obey the order.

Finally, the news comes that the battle is over, and the Confederates won. You're happy about the news, but angry that you never fired a shot. There will be other chances, though. This is just the beginning.

THE END

To follow another path, turn to page 13.
To read the conclusion, turn to page 101.

You refuse to believe the news. With one last look at the retreating soldiers, you run back toward the battle.

Soon you come upon a small Confederate force near Henry Hill. You recognize their commander, General Thomas Jackson. You can see that Jackson's men are standing steady against the Yankee attack. You join them.

Right behind you is another Confederate brigade, commanded by General Bernard Bee. His hoarse voice rises over the sound of gunfire, shouting, "Look, men! There is Jackson, standing like a stone wall. Let us determine to die here, and we will conquer. Follow me!"

In no time, the combined forces are hammering away at the Yankee troops. Slowly, you push the Union Army back.

General Thomas "Stonewall" Jackson earned his famous nickname during the battle.

Turn the page.

You don't know how long you keep fighting. You can barely see through the smoke. At one point, a Union shot hits Bee in the stomach as he rides through the battle. But you and your fellow soldiers keep firing.

By late afternoon, there are no more Yankees to shoot. The battlefield is covered with the dead and wounded. You're not sure how you survived, but you did. You drain the last drop of water from your canteen as a rider gallops toward you.

"The battle is won!" the soldier croaks. "The Union is retreating. Victory is ours!" You sink to the ground in relief. Your army has won the battle. You hope it also will win the war.

THE END

To follow another path, turn to page 13.
To read the conclusion, turn to page 101.

You turn and yell as you fire at the oncoming Yankees. Just then, a sharp pain strikes you in the upper leg. You've been shot! Blood pours from your body as you sink to the ground. The last thing you see is the glint of the sun on the bayonets of the Yankee soldiers.

THE END

To follow another path, turn to page 13.
To read the conclusion, turn to page 101.

Union soldiers gathered at Camp Sprague in Washington, D.C., before the Battle of Bull Run.

CHAPTER 3

DEFENDING THE UNION

You live in a small town in Michigan, where you work in your father's hardware store. You've never been more than 10 miles from home.

Your family is surprised that you want to enlist in the army after the attack on Fort Sumter. Your mother cries, "It's so far away. They don't need you." Father looks grim. But you are determined. Nothing is going to stop you from teaching those rebels a lesson.

45

Turn the page.

General Samuel Heintzelman
led one of the five Union
divisions at Bull Run.

You and all of your friends rush into town the next day to enlist. Before you know it, you are on a train to Washington, D.C. You know this is going to be the adventure of a lifetime.

When you arrive, you and your friends join General Samuel Heintzelman's Third Division. You've heard about Heintzelman's bravery in the Mexican War. You're looking forward to fighting under his command.

Washington, D.C., is nothing like you had imagined. The streets are muddy and filled with garbage. You and your friends spend two weeks practicing drills at camp. On July 16, your regiment gets orders to march toward Manassas Junction, Virginia. At last, you're going to war.

Turn the page.

Marching to war is much harder than you thought it would be. The few roads are narrow and pitted with holes. You trudge through scrubby fields filled with prickly thistles. At one point, you have to crawl across a log that forms a bridge over a deep ravine.

It takes your regiment three days to get to Centreville, a small town about 7 miles from Manassas Junction. You and your fellow soldiers set up camp near the town.

You're exhausted and hungry. So is everyone else. But the Confederate Army is out there, and you must be ready to fight. News comes that the army is dividing into several forces.

→If your regiment attacks the Confederates' left flank, go to page **49**.

→If your regiment heads toward the stone bridge over Bull Run creek, turn to page **58**.

General Heintzelman is planning a surprise attack on the left flank, or side, of the Confederate forces near Matthews Hill. As the Confederates march in rows, shoulder to shoulder, you'll attack them from their left. It won't be easy for the rows of soldiers to whirl around and face your attack.

To get to Matthews Hill, your regiment leaves the Warrenton Turnpike and scrambles north over a narrow, weedy path. After several hours, the path veers south. At Sudley Church, you get on the Manassas-Sudley Road.

Turn the page.

Near Matthews Hill, you're ordered to line up near a battalion of artillery. You see some soldiers dressed in colorful clothing.

"Who are they?" you ask the soldier next to you. He laughs.

"They're the Fire Zouaves, one of the most famous regiments in the Union Army," he says. "They're firefighters from New York City. I heard they helped put out a fire at the Willard Hotel in Washington, D.C., a few weeks back."

Before you have a chance to answer, you hear gunfire. The Confederates are attacking! You and the other soldiers drop behind a small hill and start returning fire.

Fire Zouaves wore a uniform of red shirts, short gray jackets, and baggy gray pants.

Turn the page.

The lack of standard uniforms made it difficult to tell Union and Confederate soldiers apart.

The heat of battle quickly surrounds you. Your ears ring from the boom of the cannons and the screams of pain from the wounded. A mixture of sweat, dirt, and gunpowder pours into your eyes, but you don't dare stop loading and firing.

You see a group of soldiers rushing toward you. It's hard to see through the smoke, but you think they're wearing blue uniforms. That doesn't help you, though. No one has matching uniforms. You have no idea if the soldiers are Union or Confederate. You feel something hit your leg, but you ignore the pain for the moment. You're too busy trying to decide what to do.

53

➤ To wait to fire on the soldiers, turn to page **54**.

➤ To fire on the soldiers, turn to page **55**.

As you hesitate, the soldiers raise their guns. Horrified, you realize that they're Confederates. You try to leap behind a tree, but the pain shoots through your wounded leg. You fall to the ground, bleeding. You pretend to be dead, hoping they'll leave you alone.

You lie still and try not to breathe as the Confederates search you. They take your rifle, your ammunition, and your food. You feel light-headed from the loss of blood.

Suddenly, you feel a lump beneath you. It's your pistol, which you shoved in your belt. You might be able to get to it.

➤ To grab your pistol, go to page 55.

➤ To continue lying still, turn to page 57.

You grab your pistol and open fire. A soldier in the front falls to the ground. To your shock, the rest turn and run. Relieved, you look down at the wound in your leg. Most of the bleeding has stopped, so you grab the shirt of a dead Confederate near you and wrap your leg. You also take his weapon and ammunition.

Your regiment has scattered, so you join a group of Union soldiers who are fighting near a small creek. You ignore the throbbing in your leg as you fire at the oncoming Confederates. You start to shake. When you try to walk, your leg buckles beneath you.

Turn the page.

The Stone House near Matthews Hill was used as a Union field hospital.

"That wound is bad," one of the soldiers says. "You need to get that looked at right away. There's a field hospital in the Stone House tavern not far from here."

You look around. The battle seems to have slowed down a bit. You might make it to the hospital. But you'd really rather keep fighting.

→To stay and fight, turn to page **62**.

→To go to the hospital, turn to page **64**.

Your trick works. The soldiers are too busy stealing your things to realize that you're still alive. With a final laugh and a kick to your side, they leave you. You lie there for a few minutes, trying to clear your head. When you finally sit up, you almost faint from the pain in your leg.

"Are you hurt, soldier?" a voice says. You look up to see a Union soldier you don't know. He's smeared with blood and dirt, just like you.

"That wound looks bad," he says. "Let's get you to a field hospital."

57

*Turn to page **62**.*

The stone bridge over Bull Run was destroyed after the battle. It was later rebuilt.

The morning of July 21 is clear and warm. You and the other soldiers forget how tired you are as you march. Some of you stop to pick and eat wild blackberries.

Soon, you see a stone bridge. Thousands of soldiers are lined up there, ready to fight. You're ordered to move upstream from the bridge and cross the creek. From there, you march to an area called Matthews Hill.

A low roar is coming from ahead of you. There, the battle has been raging for hours. Cannons explode, shaking the ground. The yells and screams of the men mix with the sound of gunfire. You raise your gun and fire at the Confederate soldiers.

The air quickly becomes black with smoke and soot. It's hard to breathe. You cough, wiping dirt and sweat from your forehead. A bullet grazes the side of your head. Blood pours down your shirt collar. You don't have time to wipe it away as you keep shooting.

Behind you, a hoarse voice yells, "Move forward!" You can't tell who is speaking. You stop, trying to hear over the battle noise.

➤To obey the order, turn to page **60**.

➤To wait, turn to page **63**.

You scramble forward, yelling at the top of your lungs. Rebels scatter. The confusion of battle is all around you. It's hard to tell which soldiers are on which side. You just fire your gun and try to stay alive.

Sometime in the early afternoon, you hear news that makes your heart glad. The Union is winning! Sure enough, many Confederates are running away. It's not over yet, though. You'll keep fighting as long as the rebels keep coming. You shoot until you run out of bullets. For a moment, you panic.

Before you can move, an officer races up on horseback. "Fall back!" he yells. "General McDowell has ordered a retreat!"

You're stunned. "Sir, do you know why?" you ask him.

General Irvin McDowell was replaced as Union commander soon after the battle.

"The rebels have reinforcements on the way," he replies before galloping away.

There's no way you and the other tired Union soldiers can fight fresh troops. Large groups of soldiers turn around and begin an orderly retreat.

➻To stay, turn to page **63**.

➻To retreat, turn to page **65**.

You're not going to let a wounded leg stop you from beating the Confederates. But just as you raise your gun, you feel a sharp pain in your right leg. You've been shot in that leg too! As you fall to the ground, the other soldier catches you.

"You're going to the hospital now. No arguments!" he tells you sternly.

You know he's right. You can't fight with two wounded legs.

*Turn to page **64**.*

You're determined to stay and fight. But as you raise your gun, you feel a sharp pain in your right leg. You look down to see the bloody bullet wound. Another soldier helps you stumble to Sudley Church, where the Union Army has set up a field hospital.

When you reach the church, you see wounded soldiers lying everywhere. Dead bodies are piled a short distance away. Your stomach churns.

A tired doctor in a bloody apron examines you. "Your bone is shattered," he says. "If I don't amputate this leg, you'll die."

63

➤To agree to the amputation, turn to page **67**.

➤To refuse, turn to page **69**.

The soldier helps you to the Stone House tavern. Someone binds your wounds with a dirty rag and gives you a sip of water.

You fall in and out of consciousness. When you wake up, it's early evening. The moans of the wounded fill the air. You call out, "What's happening?"

One of the wounded men replies, "It's a terrible day. The Confederates have won the battle. Worst of all, the army has left us here."

You fall back onto the filthy floor and close your eyes. It won't be long, you think, before the Confederates take you all prisoner. You wonder whether you'll still be alive by then.

THE END

To follow another path, turn to page 13.
To read the conclusion, turn to page 101.

Panicked Union soldiers thought the Confederates were chasing them.

You follow columns of soldiers as they leave the battlefield. Then you hear scattered gunfire behind you.

"The rebels! They're after us!" a voice shouts. The road is choked with wagons and civilians who have come out to see the battle. Panicked, the soldiers shove people out of their way.

Turn the page.

The soldiers break into a run, smashing into each other and turning over wagons and carts. You scramble out of their way. Somewhere in front of you is Washington, D.C., and safety.

After a while, you realize that the panicked soldiers were wrong. No Confederates are behind you. You walk all night. Every mile, you want to collapse, but someone grabs you and makes you keep going.

Late in the morning of the next day, you reach the outskirts of Washington. You collapse in a doorway. You vow to keep fighting for the Union. You may have lost the first battle, but you're determined not to lose the war.

THE END

To follow another path, turn to page 13.
To read the conclusion, turn to page 101.

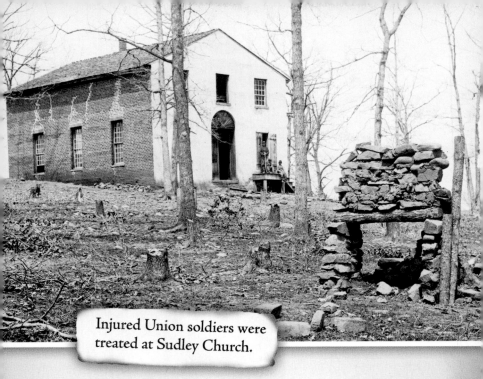

Injured Union soldiers were treated at Sudley Church.

You think for a minute, trying to ignore the pain. "Well, doc," you say finally, "I suppose I'd rather be alive with one leg than dead with two."

He nods. Another soldier grabs your arms and half-drags, half-carries you to the large tent behind the church. Several men are lying on blankets on the ground.

Turn the page.

You're lifted onto a wooden table. Another soldier puts a few drops of liquid on a cloth and then holds it to your nose and mouth. You fall unconscious.

Hours later, you start to wake up. You feel a searing pain in your leg. Someone puts a leather strap in your mouth. You bite down on it when the pain becomes unbearable. You look down to see a stump where your leg once was. You're in incredible pain. But at least you're alive.

THE END

To follow another path, turn to page 13.
To read the conclusion, turn to page 101.

There's no way you're going to let a doctor cut off your leg. "I'll take my chances, doc," you say stubbornly.

"I can't do anything for you, then," the doctor says. He gives you some medicine to help you sleep. Hours later, you awake in terrible pain. Your leg has become infected, and you are burning with fever.

As you float in and out of consciousness, you hear that the battle is over, and the Confederates won. You know you're dying, and you'll never know how the war ends.

69

THE END

To follow another path, turn to page 13.
To read the conclusion, turn to page 101.

In 1861, President Lincoln was sworn in as work was being done on the U.S. Capitol.

CHAPTER 4

WATCHING THE BATTLE

Washington, D.C., is an exciting city in 1861. Your family lives in a large home not too far from the U.S. Capitol. You've always had a comfortable life as the daughter of a successful businessman. Now, though, your world is shaken by war.

A few months ago, you heard the terrible news that Fort Sumter had been attacked. Most people laughed at the idea of the Confederacy. "This war will be over by the end of the summer," many people said. You're not so sure.

Turn the page.

The morning of July 21 is sunny and warm. You sit down to breakfast with your mother and father. The empty seat at the table reminds you that your older brother, Samuel, is gone. He enlisted in the Union Army right after the attack on Fort Sumter. His regiment marched off toward Manassas Junction a few days ago.

Everyone tries to be cheerful, but there is tension in the air. You pick up the newspaper and read about small skirmishes that have broken out between the two armies.

Father sees the look on your face and pats your hand reassuringly. "The war will probably be over by the end of the day," he says, smiling.

Mother agrees. "Those rebels don't have the stomach to fight," she says. But behind their calming words is a tone of fear.

There is a knock on your door. You're surprised to see your best friend, Abigail, and her younger brother, John.

"What are you doing out so early?" you ask.

"We're going out to watch the battle," Abigail says excitedly. "Father let us have the carriage, and we've packed a picnic lunch. Can you come with us?"

"Yes, do come," John adds. "It will be fun."

➤ *To stay home, turn to page* **74.**

➤ *To go with your friends, turn to page* **78.**

You hesitate. It would be exciting to see a real battle. But you're not sure that it would be safe.

"No, I don't think so," you say finally. "It's too dangerous. I don't want to get shot."

Abigail looks disappointed. "Mother made fried chicken. All of our friends will be there."

John nods. "Just come with us," he pleads.

But you're firm. Abigail and John climb into their carriage and drive away. You watch them go with a mixture of jealousy and fear. You don't want to go to the battle, but you don't want to be left out, either.

You climb to the small balcony on the third floor of your house and look down. You're surprised at the number of wagons and carriages on the road. More people are heading to the battle than you thought. You wonder if you made the right choice.

As it's Sunday, your family attends church as usual. It's hard to pay attention because everyone is whispering about the battle.

After the service, you and your family join other churchgoers gathered outside. Just then, your friend Elizabeth hurries past.

"Where are you going?" you ask her.

"My uncle works at the War Department," Elizabeth replies. "I'm going down there to see if there is news. Want to come with me?"

➤ To go with her, turn to page **76**.

➤ To return home, turn to page **83**.

The two of you head toward the War Department. When you arrive at the building, people are gathered near a side door. You and Elizabeth try to go in, but a guard stops you.

"Please tell us what's happening," you ask him.

"We're getting steady reports from the battle," one guard says. "The news seems good."

You and Elizabeth stay for several hours. You watch important-looking men bustle in and out all day. Every once in awhile, the guards tell you that the battle is going well.

Once, a very tall man in a black frock coat steps out. He has a tall hat perched on his head. You instantly know who he is.

"President Lincoln," you say as he passes you. "May God bless you today."

President Abraham Lincoln waited in Washington for news of the battle.

Lincoln stops and smiles at you. He reaches out to shake your trembling hand. "Thank you, young lady," he says. Then he climbs into a waiting carriage and rides down the street.

Turn to page **83**.

Watching a battle sounds exciting, so you agree to go. You're surprised at the number of wagons and elegant carriages that fill the road. You and your friends happily wave and greet everyone you pass. It feels like you're going to a carnival.

You and your friends travel to the village of Centreville. A few dozen people have settled on a grassy knoll west of town to watch the battle. One man catches your eye. There's a large box strapped on his back.

You approach him curiously. "What's that?" you ask, pointing at the box.

The man smiles and shakes your hand. "I'm Mathew Brady," he says. "This is my camera equipment. I've come to record history."

Photo taken
July 22nd
1861

BRADY
The Photographer
returned from
Bull Run

Mathew Brady was the most famous photographer of the Civil War.

Turn to page 80.

You step back, suddenly shy. Mathew Brady, the famous photographer! "It's nice to meet you," you manage to tell him before you go back to your friends.

As you unpack the lunch basket, Abigail nudges you. She points to a large, dignified man sitting nearby.

"Do you know who that is?" she whispers. "That's Senator Henry Wilson of Massachusetts. He handed out hundreds of sandwiches to the Massachusetts soldiers as they marched into battle." You're impressed to be near such an important member of Congress.

It's not long before the echo of cannon fire fills the air. Excitedly, you stand up and peer through your opera glasses at the scene a few miles away.

Everyone else is standing up too. There's so much dust and smoke that you can barely see the troops moving toward the battlefield.

Soon your ears ache from the sound of the cannon fire. You still can't see the battle. By early afternoon, you are ready to go home. But Abigail and John aren't ready to leave.

"Let's get closer, so we can see better," Abigail tells you.

To go home, turn to page **82**.

To get closer to the battle, turn to page **84**.

"No, I'm going home," you say firmly.

"Then go," Abigail says. "But I don't know how you're going to get there. You came in our carriage."

She is right. You look around helplessly until you notice your neighbors, Mr. and Mrs. Fields, preparing to leave. They agree to give you a ride home.

The journey home is a quiet one. Mrs. Fields asks you a few questions about your family, but you have little to say. You're still thinking about the battle. Before you know it, you're at your front door.

When you return home, you fall asleep in a chair. When you awake, it is early evening. Downstairs, you hear your mother crying.

You rush down the stairs. Your mother tells you the terrible news. The Union lost the battle. How could this have happened?

You run outside. Crying people are spilling out into the street. You hear that the Union Army has retreated and is headed back to the city. You wonder if your brother is all right.

"Those poor men will be hungry and injured," your mother says. "We should do something."

"We could make sandwiches and coffee for them," you say. "I'm sure they'll need help at the hospital too."

➤To help your mother make food, turn to page 86.

➤To go to the hospital, turn to page 88.

"Yes, let's go!" you say, climbing into the carriage. Slowly you bump along the road toward the battle. People have set up tables filled with food alongside the road. You wonder if it's for the soldiers or for themselves, but you don't stop to ask.

As you move closer to the battlefield, cannon fire shakes the ground like small earthquakes. The loud pop of rifles and the shouts and cries of soldiers fill the air. Men on both sides fall to the ground like rag dolls. You pray that your brother, Samuel, isn't one of them.

You stay and watch until late afternoon. It seems as if the Union is winning. You and the others cheer the soldiers as they move about the battlefield. Then, more Confederate soldiers seem to appear out of nowhere. Several groups of Union soldiers fall at once. You have a bad feeling.

Early in the battle, the Union soldiers appeared to be winning.

"Let's move farther back," you urge. "Something's not right."

"Oh, don't be such a spoilsport," Abigail says impatiently as she claps for the Union soldiers. "We're perfectly safe."

➤ *If you move back, turn to page **92**.*

➤ *If you stay, turn to page **96**.*

You and your mother stay up most of the night making piles of sandwiches and pots of strong, hot coffee. It begins to rain.

Late the next morning, soldiers begin to stumble into town. You're shocked at their appearance. They're soaked from the rain and filthy with sweat, dirt, soot, and blood. Most of them have dazed, empty expressions.

You and Mother hand out sandwiches and coffee. The men gratefully accept them. You frantically search the crowds for your brother, Samuel, but you don't see him.

You walk through the crowd until you run out of food. Tired and grief-stricken, you return home and sink down on the porch. You watch soldiers curl up on lawns, in the street, and in doorways to sleep.

You think of your brother. Is he trying to make his way back home? Or is he lying wounded somewhere? You won't let yourself think of the possibility that he may be dead. Wherever he is, you know that he'll soon face another battle.

"This is not a one-day war," you say to yourself. "This war will last a very long time."

THE END

To follow another path, turn to page 13.
To read the conclusion, turn to page 101.

You collect as much food, water, and clean bandages as you can carry and head downtown. You're not the only one who wants to help. A crowd of women is headed in the same direction that you are.

Soon you arrive at the Patent Office, where doctors have set up a makeshift hospital. You're stunned at the terrible wounds you see. Your stomach heaves at the awful sights and smells, but you swallow hard. You're determined to do whatever you can for these brave soldiers.

Soon a short woman strides up to you. "Are you here to help?" she demands.

"I want to do whatever I can," you reply. "Who are you?"

"I'm Clara Barton," the woman replies. "Come with me."

During the war, Clara Barton brought medical supplies to injured soldiers on battlefields.

Turn the page.

Military hospitals were built for injured soldiers later in the war.

You follow Clara to a huge pile of boxes. They're filled with combs, bandages, and other items.

"I've collected these for the men," she explains. "Hospitals don't have even the most basic supplies."

You and Clara spend several hours passing out the supplies to the injured soldiers. Finally, you are so tired that you sink into a corner. Clara finds you and pats your hand.

"You've done good work today," she says. "You have the makings of a fine nurse."

You sigh as you gaze sadly at the hundreds of soldiers now filling every space on the floor. You're afraid that there will be much more death and destruction to come.

THE END

To follow another path, turn to page 13.
To read the conclusion, turn to page 101.

"I don't like this," you say. "I'm going home."

"Suit yourself," Abigail says. "But you'll have to walk."

You begin to walk back the way you came. Soon the sounds of battle are behind you, but you still feel a sense of panic. Suddenly the road is filled with Union soldiers, all running toward Washington, D.C.

"We're done," one yells.

"Run for your lives," another says.

Soldiers push and shove, making you stumble forward. Panic fills the air. Your full hoop skirt makes it hard to get out of their way. You hear the sound of galloping horses behind you. A wagon full of wounded soldiers rushes past. You're shocked to see your brother, Samuel, hanging over the side of the wagon.

It was hard for women to move quickly in the full hoop skirts of the 1860s.

Turn the page.

"Stop!" you call. The wagon slows down enough for you to climb aboard.

"Sister, I'm so glad you're here," Samuel whispers. As you cradle Samuel's head in your lap, you see a deep wound in his shoulder. Swallowing hard, you pray that he'll get to Washington in time.

The ride is bumpy and miserable. Flies buzz around the men's open wounds. You do your best to swat them away. Several men die along the way, but Samuel is still alive. When you get to town, you ask the driver to take you home. The carriage pulls up in front of your house.

"Help!" you scream, and your parents appear at the door. Your mother sobs as you help your father carry Samuel into the house. You clean Samuel's wounds and make him comfortable.

Samuel's wounds are serious. He was shot in the shoulder and in the leg. But the bullets went cleanly through his flesh. As the night wears on, you're relieved to see that there is no sign of infection.

You and your mother tend to Samuel all night. By dawn, it appears he will live. You're happy for Samuel, but sad for all the soldiers who died that day. You know this battle is just the beginning of the long, bloody war to come.

THE END

To follow another path, turn to page 13.
To read the conclusion, turn to page 101.

You're sure that the Union forces will turn the battle around, so you decide to stay. Soon, however, it's clear that the Confederates are winning. You hear that General McDowell has ordered a retreat. The road begins to fill with rows of soldiers marching back to Washington.

You, Abigail, and John join the mob of carriages, wagons, and soldiers crowding the narrow road. Gunfire echoes behind you.

"They're after us!" a soldier yells.

The crowd panics. People rush madly away from the battlefield. You and your friends are caught up in the confusion. Abigail tries to urge the frightened horses forward, but they stop in their tracks.

Without warning, a group of soldiers overtakes your carriage. "What are you doing?" you cry.

"These men are hurt. They can't walk any longer," their leader says. Another soldier roughly hauls you out of your seat and throws you onto the dusty road. Abigail and John fall beside you. The soldiers jump into your carriage and disappear into the crowd.

Nearby, you see Senator Wilson riding bareback on a horse. As he struggles to stay on, he yells, "The Confederates shot at my wagon and tried to kill me!"

You can't believe that the Union soldiers left you to be trampled by the mob. You see tables full of food overturned by the side of the road. Hungry, dirty soldiers are grabbing everything they can. The gunfire from behind you pushes you onward with the crowds.

Turn the page.

Senator Henry Wilson was an onlooker at the battle. Later, he served as U.S. vice president.

Late the next morning, you and your friends finally reach the outskirts of Washington. Your feet are throbbing from the long walk. You're shocked at the sight that greets you. Hundreds of wounded, dirty soldiers fill the streets. You turn toward home, tired and filled with sadness. You realize that this war is going to last a long time.

THE END

To follow another path, turn to page 13.
To read the conclusion, turn to page 101.

Inexperienced soldiers caused confusion during the Battle of Bull Run.

CHAPTER 5

THE FIRST BATTLE

The Battle of Bull Run was disorganized. Some of the soldiers were trained members of the army. But many on both sides were civilian volunteers. These men had only a short time to learn how to fight before the battle. Their inexperience caused much confusion on the battlefield.

Uniforms were another cause of confusion. At later battles, Confederate soldiers wore gray uniforms. Union soldiers wore blue. At Bull Run, though, soldiers didn't have matching uniforms. Sometimes they didn't know if they were facing enemy soldiers or members of their own army.

Misinformation also played a part in the battle. When Confederate forces were driven back to Henry Hill, Union General McDowell thought his army had won. Some Confederate soldiers heard this news and started retreating.

Late in the day, Confederate reinforcements arrived. The reinforcements didn't outnumber the Union forces. But many Union soldiers saw the fresh Confederates and thought their army was beaten. Union troops began to retreat.

At first, the retreat was calm. But soon rumors that the Confederates were chasing them spread through the Union soldiers. The retreat became a riot. But by that time, the Confederates were too disorganized to chase the Union troops. About 2,000 Union soldiers and 1,700 Confederate soldiers died in the battle.

Lee surrendered to Grant in the village of Appomattox Court House, Virginia.

Bull Run was the first major battle of a bloody four-year war. The Civil War claimed the lives of about 620,000 people. It is the deadliest war in U.S. history.

The Confederates won Bull Run and several other early battles. But by 1863, the Union was winning. On April 9, 1865, Confederate General Robert E. Lee surrendered to Union General Ulysses S. Grant. The war was over at last.

The Civil War changed the United States in many ways. Slavery became illegal. Thousands of African Americans suddenly found themselves without homes, jobs, or money. Some moved to large Northern cities. Others became pioneers and headed west. Most stayed in the South and lived in conditions that weren't much better than when they were slaves.

The war destroyed many parts of the South, including the cities of Atlanta, Georgia, and Richmond, Virginia. Rebuilding was slow and difficult. Some areas never fully recovered.

The war also settled the question of whether states had a right to secede. Before the war, state governments believed they had the right to do whatever they pleased.

Much of Richmond, Virginia, was destroyed at the end of the war.

The war united the states in a way that had not been possible before. It was clear that no state had the right to leave the Union. The Civil War gave the country a sense of unity and purpose.

Time Line

November 1860 — Abraham Lincoln is elected president of the United States.

December 20, 1860 — South Carolina is the first Southern state to secede from the Union.

January–June 1861 — Mississippi, Florida, Alabama, Georgia, Louisiana, Texas, Virginia, Arkansas, North Carolina, and Tennessee secede. They, along with South Carolina, form the Confederacy.

April 12, 1861 — Confederates fire the first shots of the Civil War when they attack Fort Sumter.

July 16 — Union General Irvin McDowell's army marches toward Manassas Junction. The Confederate Army of the Potomac, under the command of General Pierre Beauregard, is already there.

July 18 —Union and Confederate soldiers fight a small skirmish at Blackburn's Ford.

July 21

2:30 a.m. — More Confederate soldiers arrive by train at Manassas Junction; McDowell's army begins the march toward Beauregard's Confederate forces.

5:30 a.m. — Union forces arrive at the stone bridge and take up positions.

6:00 a.m. — The battle begins.

8:30 a.m. — Confederate forces are ordered to Matthews Hill to block the Union Army.

10:30 a.m. — Several Union and Confederate brigades fight fiercely on Matthews Hill.

11:30 a.m. — After heavy fighting, the Confederates are forced to retreat from Matthews Hill. The Confederates seem to be losing the battle.

12:00 p.m. — Confederate units rush to attack the Union troops at Henry Hill.

1:00 p.m. — Several Union brigades retreat from Henry Hill.

2:30 p.m. — The Confederates capture Union cannons on Henry Hill. More Union forces retreat.

4:00 p.m. — Union brigades try to attack Henry Hill, but are defeated.

6:00 p.m. — The Union Army retreats. The Confederates win the battle.

April 9, 1865 — After four years of war, Confederate General Robert E. Lee surrenders at Appomattox Court House, Virginia.

OTHER PATHS TO EXPLORE

In this book, you've seen how the events of the Battle of Bull Run look different from three points of view.

Perspectives on history are as varied as the people who lived it. You can explore other paths on your own to learn more about what happened. Seeing history from many points of view is an important part of understanding it.

Here are some ideas for other Battle of Bull Run points of view to explore:

◆ Several families lived near the site of the battle. What was that experience like?

◆ Many people had family members or friends who fought on or supported the opposite side. How do you think these relationships affected people's actions during the war?

◆ If the Confederacy had won the war, what do you think life for people in this country would have been like?

READ MORE

Anderson, Maxine. *Great Civil War Projects You Can Build Yourself.* White River Junction, Vt.: Nomad Press, 2005.

DeFord, Deborah H. *The Civil War.* Milwaukee: World Almanac Library, 2007.

Poulakidas, Georgene. *The Civil War.* New York: PowerKids Press/Primary Source, 2006.

Vierow, Wendy. *The Battle of Bull Run: Confederate Forces Overwhelm Union Troops.* New York: PowerKids Press, 2004.

INTERNET SITES

FactHound offers a safe, fun way to find Internet sites related to this book. All of the sites on FactHound have been researched by our staff.

109

Here's how:
1. Visit *www.facthound.com*
2. Choose your grade level.
3. Type in this book ID **1429620110** for age-appropriate sites. You may also browse subjects by clicking on letters, or by clicking on pictures and words.
4. Click on the **Fetch It** button.

FactHound will fetch the best sites for you!

GLOSSARY

artillery (ar-TI-luhr-ee) — cannons and other large guns used during battles

bayonet (BAY-uh-nuht) — a long metal blade attached to the end of a rifle or musket

brigade (bri-GAYD) — a unit of soldiers that includes two or more regiments

Confederacy (kuhn-FE-druh-see) — the 11 Southern states that left the United States to form the Confederate States of America

courier (KUR-ee-ur) — a person who delivers important messages

rebel (REB-uhl) — a person who fights against a government; Confederate soldiers were called rebels during the Civil War.

110

regiment (REJ-uh-muhnt) — a unit of soldiers that includes two or more battalions

secede (si-SEED) — to formally withdraw from a group or organization

skirmish (SKUR-mish) — a minor fight during a war

surrender (suh-REN-dur) — to give up or admit defeat in battle

BIBLIOGRAPHY

Davis, William C. *Battle at Bull Run: A History of the First Major Campaign of the Civil War.* Garden City, N.Y.: Doubleday, 1977.

Detzer, David. *Donnybrook: The Battle of Bull Run, 1861.* Orlando, Fla.: Harcourt, 2004.

Editors of Time-Life Books. *First Manassas.* Alexandria, Va.: Time-Life Books, 1997.

Making of America — The War of the Rebellion http://cdl.library.cornell.edu/moa/browse.monographs/ waro.html

PBS — The Civil War http://www.pbs.org/civilwar/war

Rafuse, Ethan S. *A Single Grand Victory: The First Campaign and Battle of Manassas.* Wilmington, Del.: SR Books, 2002.

U.S. Army Center of Military History http://www.army.mil/cmh/StaffRide/1st%20Bull%20 Run/Overview.htm

Wheeler, Richard. *A Rising Thunder: From Lincoln's Election to the Battle of Bull Run: An Eyewitness History.* New York: HarperCollins, 1994.

INDEX